A journey *of* discovery

ON THE ROAD WITH JESUS' FOLLOWERS

A journey *of* discovery

ON THE ROAD WITH JESUS' FOLLOWERS

Kate Hayes

A journey of discovery: on the road with Jesus' followers

An individual or small group Bible resource from Scripture Union

Scripture Union, 207–209 Queensway, Bletchley, MK2 2EB, England, UK
Email: info@scriptureunion.org.uk
Website: www.scriptureunion.org.uk

ISBN: 978 1 84427 180 1

Scripture Union Australia
Locked Bag 2, Central Coast Business Centre, NSW 2252
www.su.org.au

First published in the UK by Scripture Union, 2005, Reprinted 2007

Scripture taken from the New Living Translation, British text, published by Tyndale House Publishers, Inc., Wheaton, Illinois, USA, and distributed by STL Ltd., Carlisle, Cumbria, England.

British Library Cataloguing-in-Publication data

A catalogue record for this book is available from the British Library.

Cover design: Philip Grundy
Internal design and typesetting by Servis Filmsetting Ltd, Manchester
Printed in China by 1010 Printing International Ltd

Scripture Union is an international Christian charity working with churches in more than 130 countries, providing resources to bring the good news about Jesus Christ to children, young people and families and to encourage them to develop spiritually through the Bible and prayer.

As well as our network of volunteers, staff and associates who run holidays, church-based events and school Christian groups, we produce a wide range of publications and support those who use our resources through training programmes.

The way ahead

*T*his book is for anyone, as an individual or with a small group, who wants to grow in their understanding of the journey taken by Jesus' followers and its significance for us today. None of us experience exactly the same journey, although some will find themselves on paths that others have travelled. It's good to meet fellow travellers along the way and learn from each other.

If we look back over the past few years, some will be able to pick out moments of significant life-change, events that completely altered routines, maybe even expectations or priorities. Others may see nothing of the kind, looking back on familiar patterns, familiar hopes and attitudes. Whatever the experiences of our recent past, we all know that anything can change in an instant.

In this series, we focus on the journey of one small group whose lives were utterly changed after the unexpected arrival of one man. Certainly Peter and the others remain recognisably themselves throughout the New Testament, but as time passes they are no longer involved in their everyday occupations. Instead they become preachers and teachers, people enabled to heal miraculously, to be courageous witnesses for Jesus and the foundation stones of a rapidly growing church. Such a transformation wasn't something they had expected or planned for, but is triggered simply through making the decision to follow Jesus and by journeying with him.

Such significant change wasn't primarily brought about through increasing their scriptural knowledge, or even through the hours they spent in the temple and the synagogues in worship, but first and foremost through the time they spent with Jesus himself. This exposure brought them new attitudes, new priorities and a new way of thinking about the world. As they continued to follow Jesus they realised that they had been given a part to play in God's purposes and the gifts to carry it out.

Such transformation isn't restricted to the pages of the New Testament. We too have the same opportunity to know Jesus and to experience his impact on our lives. As followers of Jesus we share the disciples' call to bring the good news of Jesus to the world around us, and the opportunity to be changed by him into people who can do just that.

Jesus' disciples had a particular role in beginning the church and the advantage of knowing Jesus on earth, but they were still travellers like us, facing the same complications and questions that we do. As we follow their journey with Jesus we find a guide to the challenges of our own lives; signposts that will help us discover the place and purpose that Jesus has for us too.

The Solitary Traveller

This book is a companion for the solitary traveller. You can work through the material at your own pace, ignoring only those sections marked with the group logo. It may be helpful for you to record your thoughts along the way, either on the pages or in a separate notebook.

The Group of Travellers

This book is also a companion for the small group. You may have come together with a Christian friend, as a prayer triplet, as an existing small fellowship group, or as part of a group specially convened for Lent or some other season of the year. Decide whether one person will lead each time you meet, or whether a different person will lead each session. You may want to skip those sections marked with the solitary traveller logo.

Using the material

The material is divided into six sessions or chapters and there is a consistent pattern to the material in each.

Setting Out will ease you gently into the focus of the session through some fun questions or activities. Don't skip this part, even if you are a solitary traveller, because however light this material seems it will flag up some important attitudes and preconceptions and will prepare you for deeper exploration of some key issues. Within the group setting, this opening time will develop relationships and encourage honest sharing which will ultimately help the group to be more comfortable in praying together.

Signposts will take you into the Bible. This time of discovery alone or together will open up a number of lines of thought as you follow through the questions. For groups, this section will particularly encourage discussion and the sharing of experiences.

Prayer is the next section, during which time there is opportunity to pray in a way that relates to the focus of the session so far. Don't be tempted to rush this; it is just as important as the rest of the session.

Finally, there is a **Further Afield** section. This allows further exploration of related issues in the Bible. Depending on how long you have together, groups wanting to lengthen the Bible study section could use some or all of this material in the **Signposts** section. If time is limited, group members might like to use **Further Afield** at home for personal study during the week. Individuals can choose to use some or all of this section.

1 Come, Follow Me

*P*eaceful. Predictable. Is that what you want your life to be, or do you love variety, new things every day? Maybe you're the kind of person that embraces change, new ideas and new things. Or maybe you're the one hiding at the back, hoping it will all go back to normal soon. Before the disciples met Jesus, they could have been living quiet, contented lives; or they could have been dissatisfied, seeking something new. Whatever their situation, whatever their preferences, from the moment Jesus invited them to join him, life would never be the same again.

Setting Out

Q: The person leading the service unexpectedly asks for a volunteer to come to the front. They don't explain why. Do you:

- hide under your seat;

- leap up and run forward;

- try to look keen but make sure you can't be seen round the very tall bloke in front of you;

- start chanting the very tall bloke's name so the leader picks them, not you;

- sneak out and never return?

Q: You're checking in at the airport after a week away when it's announced the flight is overbooked and volunteers are needed to fly tomorrow instead. They're offering a free night in a four star hotel with all meals and £100 each in cash. Do you:

- start shouting – you've paid and they're duty bound to get you on that plane;

- hold out in the hope the offer will get even better;

- elbow a little old lady out of the way in your haste to accept;

- mutter loudly, trying to shame the man in front into accepting the offer so you'll get his seat;

- chill out? Whatever will be will be. If you get on, great; if you don't, at least you'll make some money out of it.

Q: The company you work for have developed a vaccine against the common cold and they're looking for staff volunteers to test it. They don't anticipate any side-effects but . . . Do you:

- ignore them;

- arrange an immediate all-day meeting, far away;

- offer at once – it's a noble cause after all;

- offer if the deal is right;

- suggest they ask that young chap in the next office? He won't mind if he develops green pustules and all his hair falls out, will he?

Q: Did you respond to these scenarios in roughly the same way each time or not? Why was that?

A well-known cartoon shows an army sergeant seeking a volunteer from the men in front of him. Everybody but one takes a step back, leaving the remaining man looking as though he has actively volunteered for the job. The implication is that volunteering is dangerous!

We may well be wary of signing up for something when we don't know exactly what is going to be involved. Perhaps we just don't quite trust the person doing the asking. Sometimes we worry we'll end up looking silly or find ourselves stuck with the most boring task possible. Most people just don't like taking a leap in the dark. Are you willing to volunteer when you don't know quite what you're getting into? What makes you a keen volunteer? And what makes you step back quickly?

Signposts

Read

Luke 5:1–11: Jesus and the fishermen

Jesus commandeers Simon's boat so he can preach more effectively to the crowds, and Simon cooperates. Then, afterwards, something slightly strange happens: Jesus doesn't get out, thank Simon and go on his way, but instead directs him to get back out onto the lake and fish.

Q: Imagine you're planning a fishing trip and you seek advice on when and where to fish. Two suggestions are offered, one from an experienced local fisherman, the other from a non-fishing carpenter who lives in a town some miles away. Whose advice would you be most likely to follow? Why?

Q: We've probably all experienced moments when someone has tried to tell us how to do something we can already do pretty well. How do you feel when that happens to you? Can you remember a specific occasion? How did you respond to that person?

Q: Simon and his colleagues have just been up all night fishing without any success. How do you think he felt when Jesus told him to go back out on the lake?

Q: Why do you think Simon didn't just give Jesus the brush off?

Whatever Simon really felt about Jesus' suggestion, he goes along with it and fish flood the boat. After this we might expect him to be leaping up and down shrieking with excitement, trying to sign Jesus up as a partner in the business or even arguing that it was just a fluke. Instead, Simon drops to his knees, suddenly conscious of his sinfulness.

Q: Why did this experience make Simon feel this way?

Q: What do you think that day taught Simon about Jesus?

Q: What does this event teach us about Simon's character?

Jesus didn't line up the fishermen and ask for volunteer disciples to step forward. He's more particular than that. His strategy is to seek out potential followers and invite them to be his disciples, to come and follow him. The moment the fishermen accept their lives change completely. Their decision was certainly a leap in the dark, apparently made on the spur of the moment; they can't possibly have really understood what lay ahead of them. What was it that led them to make such a life-changing decision?

Jesus was particular about who he asked to be a disciple but his choices were not always obvious. The fishermen were not particularly well-educated, well connected or even well prepared for what was to come. However, they did have one advantage over other potential disciples: they were apparently respectable men, living in the heart of their community. Not all of Jesus' disciples even had that.

Read

Luke 5:27–32: Jesus and the Taxman

In stark contrast to the fishermen, Levi was never going to be a valued member of his community. The tax collectors were social outcasts, collaborators with the hated Roman occupiers, lining their pockets at the expense of their own people, the ordinary Jews.

Q: How did the Pharisees respond to the idea of mixing with taxmen and others like them? Why was that?

Against all expectations of how a 'proper' religious leader should behave, Jesus not only speaks directly to Levi, he goes and eats with him, and his friends, at a party and finally asks him to be his disciple too.

If Levi had had to fill in a job application for the post of disciple, he might have been tempted to skip over the details of his current job and lifestyle but when Jesus calls Levi he never mentions these things at all.

Q: Why do you think that was?

Q: So if Jesus didn't mention his job why then did Levi immediately give it up?

Q: Levi doesn't seem to be an obvious candidate for the Messiah's disciple. What was it about Levi that led Jesus to choose him?

Q: Surely it would have been much more sensible to ask the Pharisees? They already had a lot of knowledge and experience in 'religious' things. Why didn't Jesus approach them to be his disciples too?

In choosing these people, Jesus wasn't implying that qualifications or experience were barriers to discipleship or that a dodgy lifestyle was a good thing! Instead Jesus was demonstrating that anyone whose heart was open to him could follow him.

Q: How do we know that Simon Peter and the other fishermen met this requirement? And what about Levi?

EXPECTATIONS AND REALITY

Q: Imagine you asked friends or colleagues who don't go to church what they think churchgoers are like. What do you think they would say? How might they expect people to look? Or behave?

Q: How does this picture match up with the real people who go to your church?

Q: If these pictures are different why do you think that is?

Q: Jesus made it clear that anyone could be his disciple. Do you think that our churches really believe that is true?

Q: How is that shown in the daily life of your church?

Q: We need to make sure that those currently outside the church also know that truth. Imagine someone who has never been to church before comes to your main Sunday service. How easy would it be for them to follow what was happening? What would they find confusing?

Q: What could your church do to make your services easier for outsiders and newcomers to follow?

Q: Now imagine this visitor is very different from the majority of your congregation, perhaps from a different age group or cultural background, dressed more casually or chatting with their companion when everyone else is quiet. How do you think people would react? Would they feel welcome? How could the church make them feel part of the church family?

WHAT ABOUT ME?

Jesus made it clear that it is what is inside us, the state of our heart, that makes us his true followers. Even so, Christians can find themselves trusting in other things instead; maybe Jesus will love me more if I improve my Bible knowledge, or I take on yet another new role in church or work longer hours or never complain about anything.

Q: Why do you think people try to earn Jesus' favour through good deeds?

Q: Do you find yourself falling into this trap? If so, what do you hope will put you in his 'good books'?

Paul says, 'For if you are trying to make yourselves right with God by keeping the law, you have been cut off from Christ! You have fallen away from God's grace' (Galatians 5:4). His words remind us that our position as followers of Jesus is as a result of grace – our acceptance of God's free gift – and not of anything we achieve for ourselves.

FINALLY, CALLED FOR A PURPOSE

Jesus didn't want disciples so he could feel good about having many followers. Instead they were an essential part of God's plan, the people who would spread his message far and wide. The first hint of that purpose comes right at the beginning, as Jesus calls Simon to become a fisher of men. Like Simon we aren't chosen to make up numbers, but to play our vital part in God's purposes for the world today.

The first disciples were eventually very clear about their part in God's plans. For many today, that just isn't the case.

Q: How can someone without a sense of a clear call still play a vital part in God's purposes?

Q: Are you clear about your part in God's plan or not?

Q: However you answered, how does your life show that you are playing your part today?

Prayer

The study may have raised questions or issues that people would like to pray for. If so, offer the opportunity to share these things with one another, then pray together, either in silence or in open prayer, as you prefer.

End with one person reading these sentences aloud. Allow time for quiet prayer and reflection between each line.

Lord Jesus we know that whatever is in our past, today you offer us forgiveness and a new beginning.

Give us courage and strength and determination to turn away from the wrong things in our lives and to live God's way from now on.

Show us what it really means to put you first in our lives, to put your priorities above our own.

May we be your wholehearted followers, playing our full part in God's plans for the world.

Further Afield

1 RIGHT ATTITUDES

Read

Luke 18:9–14

Appearances can be deceptive! The Pharisee did many good deeds and lived in obedience to God's laws, the taxman did not. Jesus' listeners might well have assumed the Pharisee was closest to God's heart but he makes it clear that isn't so.

Q: What words would sum up the attitudes of these two men in the temple?

Q: What does the Pharisee need to do in order to be made right with God?

Q: Are there times when you are tempted to behave like the Pharisee? Perhaps you could ask God to show you if that is sometimes the case. End by using the words of the tax-collector as a prayer for God's mercy on you.

2 THE GOOD NEWS IS FOR EVERYONE

Read

Luke 8:1–3

Overlooked, pushed aside, socially restricted. It wasn't always easy being a woman in Jesus' day, and that didn't change in religious circles. However, anyone could be a follower of Jesus and everyone had a part to play.

Q: Do you find yourself doing 'backroom' tasks? If so how do you feel about them? How do you deal with the days nobody seems to notice, or care, that you've worked hard?

Q: Do you find yourself in 'upfront' roles? If so, how do you feel about that? Are you ever at risk of thinking you are more important than the backroom workers?

Q: Whether we are at the front or behind the scenes, we all benefit from knowing our contributions are appreciated. Think about the people you know. Do you thank them for their efforts? How could you show your appreciation of them?

3 OUR RESPONSE TO JESUS

Read

Luke 19:1–10

Do you know anyone who's been to a royal garden party? To get in to such an exclusive event you need an invitation, which depends on your noble deeds, then you have to meet the strict dress standards and then to stay in I expect you have to behave moderately well too! Even after all that, you still might not get to meet your host.

Here we read about a tea party with a difference. The host isn't prepared, doesn't have any noble deeds on his conscience and isn't even the one offering the invitation.

Q: Why do you think Jesus picked out Zacchaeus to be his host?

Q: How did Jesus' visit change Zacchaeus?

Q: When we experience Jesus' forgiveness we can forget about our sins and try to put things right as far as we can. Are there areas of your life where you would be better trying to put things right? What would be a wise way to do that? Do you need to find someone to help you do this?

2 *Growth*

*T*he twelve are chosen and now begin the process of learning just what it means to be a disciple. One day the first responsibility for sharing Jesus' message with the wider world will fall on them. The problem is that they know and understand so little! And they are frustratingly human: easily distracted; slow to learn; slow to change. How is Jesus going to teach them everything they need to know in such a short time?

Setting Out

You've been chosen to play the solo part in a trumpet concerto at the Albert Hall in London in six months' time. There's just one small problem: you've got the trumpet but you can't play it – yet. Time and money are limited so you must keep your training costs down.

Q: Which of these do you think would prepare you most effectively and why?

- Regular lessons and daily practice fitted around your ordinary job.
- Arranging a week's holiday just before the concert and taking a crash course – lessons all day every day in that time.
- Buying the best book available on playing the trumpet and reading it carefully.
- Asking a really great trumpet player for advice on how to play the piece.

Q: How do you prefer to learn new things (whether you want to or not)?

- Regular lessons with a teacher.
- Working it out, hit or miss, on your own.
- A good book that explains it all bit by bit.
- Something else. What?

Q: Does your preferred method work for every kind of skill or not? What might you find hard to learn this way?

Signposts

Read

Luke 6:12–16

Jesus has chosen his inner circle of disciples, the twelve. Why 12, and not just two or three?

From this moment, their training programme begins. We know that if they had taken a test at this moment they'd have shown that they didn't really understand who Jesus was, what he was doing or what would happen to them in the future. If they are going to play their full part in God's purposes then they certainly have a great deal to learn.

Jesus could have taught his disciples in many different ways:

- they could have had themed teaching sessions followed by essays for homework;
- they could have had daily Scripture studies with discussion questions;
- he could have given them a training manual for them to work through on their own at home.

Instead, we see him mostly using a very different method.

THE MASTER'S TRAINING PROGRAMME

Growing as disciples involved:

1 Spending time together

If some of the disciples were naturally solitary people it seems likely that they found being a disciple difficult from time to time. Why? Because almost every mention of the disciples in the Gospels refers to them together, as a full group, as 'the disciples' or 'the twelve', or occasionally as a smaller group.

Q: How could spending time together actively help the disciples to grow as followers of Jesus?

Q: How might Jesus have benefited from travelling with the 12 disciples too?

Q: Have you had experience of being helped to follow Jesus by being part of a group? Why do you think that was?

2 Spending time with Jesus

Have you ever done a job that required you to live in or be available, perhaps on-call, for long hours through the day and night? Are there any advantages to this kind of working over normal nine-to-five type hours? What are the advantages of shorter or fixed working hours?

The post of disciple definitely didn't fit into a tidy working pattern. In three years with Jesus there's no mention of a disciple being off on holiday, or receiving a bonus for working a long day. Being one of the twelve was a whole time, whole life commitment. As a consequence they spent a huge amount of time with Jesus, travelling, eating, talking and watching him, all day, every day, through all the ordinary moments of life, and it was often through these daily experiences that Jesus taught them about being his followers. For example:

Read

Luke 7:11–17

Imagine you were one of the disciples.

Q: How do you think you would have felt when the young man sat up?

Q: Jesus raised the young man from the dead, as he raised Lazarus (John 11) and Jairus' daughter (Luke 8). However, he didn't raise every dead person he came across. Why do you think that was?

Q: As he didn't raise everybody, what was the point of raising this particular person?

Q: What did this incident teach the disciples about Jesus?

Read

Luke 8:22–25

Q: Another ordinary day with Jesus. This isn't a planned teaching session, and yet it becomes a learning experience for the disciples. The disciples had seen Jesus' power at work before. Why do you think they were so afraid during the storm?

Q: The disciples react to this experience with awe and amazement. Why do you think they found it so amazing that Jesus could control the wind and the waves when they had already seen him raise someone from the dead?

Q: Fear seems a pretty normal reaction under the circumstances, doesn't it? The danger, we're told, is real and Jesus is asleep and yet he rebukes them for it. Is it always wrong to feel fear?

Q: Can you think of situations where fear would show we, too, aren't putting our trust in Jesus?

Q: Jesus could have told the disciples about his power over death and over nature but here they saw that for themselves. Why do you think this was an effective way for them to learn more about Jesus?

Learning from a book wouldn't have been enough for the disciples. Knowledge is important, but the priority was for them to know Jesus, to build a relationship with him, so they learned best by spending time with him. In his presence they saw him at work, saw how he related to people, discovered his character and habits and from that learned how his followers should be too. It was a wonderful position to be in: Jesus himself says to the disciples, 'How privileged you are to see what you have seen. I tell you, many prophets and kings have longed to see and hear what you have seen and heard, but they could not' (Luke 10:23b,24).

However, if the best way to learn to be a disciple, to get to know Jesus, is to spend time with him, then there's something that makes this apparently much more difficult for us than for the twelve.

WE CAN'T SEE AND MEET THE PHYSICAL JESUS

Q: Have you ever had the experience of close friends moving away? If so, how easy was it to keep that friendship strong? Was the friendship then different from the way it had been before?

Q: Wouldn't it be good to meet Jesus in person, in a human form? Or do you think it would be scary? How would you feel if he walked into the room now?

Q: The disciples had the privilege of seeing and speaking to Jesus in person everyday, an experience we can't have in this life. How then can we possibly build a relationship with him? Is it possible for our relationship with Jesus ever to be as strong as the disciples had with him?

Q: What kind of things might people find difficult about getting to know Jesus when they can't meet him in human form? Which of these, if any, do you find a problem? If you are meeting as a group, does anyone have a possible solution, a way of overcoming this?

Q: The twelve were also fortunate to be able to leave their homes and jobs behind to be with Jesus. Luke tells us that some of the women were so committed to Jesus that they contributed their money to support both him and his disciples (Luke 8:3). Many of us need to earn money and/or have caring responsibilities so it isn't possible or necessary for everyone to do the same. However, imagine all other distractions were removed from your life for a while. Do you think there would be other things, things about yourself, which would still make such a wholehearted commitment difficult to sustain?

So, we can't see Jesus in person and most of us have other commitments that need our attention. Is it possible then for us to be true disciples or should we give up now? It may not always be obvious to us but we have some advantages over the first disciples.

1 We have God's Word

Read
2 Timothy 3:16,17

The disciples learnt about Jesus as they went along, with all the confusions and misunderstandings that went with that. They didn't know what was going to happen in the future and even when Jesus tried to explain they either didn't really listen or didn't really understand. In contrast, we are privileged to know the end of the story. The Bible spells out for us who Jesus was, the purpose of his death and resurrection and God's plans for his people. We can see the bigger picture. The disciples had to start from scratch and build up understanding slowly; for us it is as though we have already done half the course.

Q: How does God's Word help us to be his disciples?

Q: Obviously it isn't going to do that if we leave our Bibles closed up on a shelf. How often do you read God's Word for yourself? What do you find difficult about doing that? What have you found helps to make this easier for you?

2 We have the Holy Spirit

Read

2 Corinthians 1:21,22 and 3:18

Q: We have another gift from God, the Holy Spirit. How does he help us grow as disciples of Jesus?

The key to being a follower of Jesus is becoming like him, having his priorities and living his way. We may not have the embodied Jesus with us everyday, but we do have God's Word and God's Spirit to help us on the way.

FINALLY: KEEPING IN TOUCH

Q: Do you use text messages? If so, do you think they help to build your relationships or not? Why?

One advantage, and maybe disadvantage, of texting is that it offers instant contact with someone pretty much wherever they might be and whatever they are doing. Such contact, used wisely, can help to build and deepen a relationship with someone. Of course we can't text Jesus, but we can stay in constant and immediate contact with him too, contact that doesn't rely on a strong signal or sufficient battery power. That contact is, of course, prayer. Jesus may not be with us physically but he is still always available to us.

Q: Would you describe your prayer life as:

- non-existent;
- occasional emergency messages;
- one-way conversations but lots of them;
- long chats, involving speaking and listening;
- other? What?

Q: What kind of prayer life would most effectively build someone's relationship with Jesus do you think? Why?

Q: What advice would you give to someone who felt they had a less than ideal prayer life who now wanted to start developing a richer prayer relationship with Jesus?

Being a follower, a disciple, of Jesus is first and foremost about growing more like him; a process that depends on building a relationship with him. As that grows, our priorities change, his priorities becoming ours. Next time we'll look at some of the priorities that should be the mark of a true disciple.

Prayer

Some groups might like to have a few small mirrors available or even one large one. Others might prefer to use their imagination. Have one person read the words in italics below whilst the others listen. Allow time for reflection where that seems appropriate.

Have everyone either look into a mirror or imagine doing so.

Sometimes our face reflects our lifestyle. We can look well or tanned or maybe tired and drawn.

Sometimes our face reflects the reality of life. We may have lines or marks of ageing, there may be scars or temporary marks from glasses.

Sometimes our face reflects our personality or our feelings. We may look angry or sad, show apprehension or uncertainty.

What does your face reflect about you today?

Allow a pause for reflection then read the following verse:

'And all of us have had that veil removed so that we can be mirrors that brightly reflect the glory of the Lord. And as the Spirit of the Lord works within us, we become more and more like him and reflect his glory even more'. (2 Corinthians 3:18)

Put the mirrors down then read all or part of Psalm 103, a psalm that reminds us what God is like.

God's glory isn't just reflected in our faces but in our whole selves, in our lifestyles and relationships.

As the Spirit of the Lord works in us, we become more and more like him.

Who am I becoming? Do I reflect God's glory to others?

End by all saying the following words together:

Lord, we give ourselves to you. Work in us that we may become like you, reflecting your glory to others.

Further Afield

1 STEPPING OUT

Read

Luke 9:1–6,10

Following Jesus wasn't just about sitting back and watching. After a while the twelve found themselves out and involved in ministry despite their inexperience and lack of full understanding. They were expected to put what they had seen and heard into practice.

Q: Do you think Jesus was taking a risk sending the twelve out in this way, or not?

Q: Why do you think Jesus wanted them to do this?

Q: What were the benefits of reporting back to Jesus afterwards?

Q: What could these verses teach us about the best way for people to get involved in ministry?

Q: What about you? Are you putting what you learn into practice?

2 GROWTH IS A SLOW PROCESS

Read

Luke 9:11–17 and 43b–50

The twelve might have been out ministering without Jesus but they still had much to learn.

Despite seeing Jesus work amazing miracles they believed that feeding five thousand people would be impossible; they didn't understand Jesus' teaching and were too afraid to ask him to explain. Their quarrelling shows that their character was very definitely still a work in progress. Not a great record, is it!

Q: How did Jesus respond to the disciples' imperfections? Why do you think that was?

Q: Like them, we too are a work in progress aren't we? Which areas of your life are growing more slowly than you'd like?

Q: How do you respond to your own imperfections? Or how about the imperfections and slow growth of others?

Pray for yourself and for those around you. Pray for the desire to grow, the openness to learn and the patience to live with the often slow pace of change!

3 COUNTING THE COST

Read

Luke 9:57–62 and 14:25–35

At first reading, these two passages seem to say that following Jesus involves ignoring the demands of our existing responsibilities and relationships. However, a far more likely explanation is that Jesus was pointing to the tendency for excuses; people wanted to wait for perfect conditions before committing themselves fully to him.

Q: Are you waiting for something to change before you obey Jesus? Sometimes that can be a wise move, at other times it is an excuse. Which is it for you? How do you know? Who do you know who offers wise advice? What would they say?

The other point here is to show the cost of following Jesus and remind us to consider that cost carefully before making a commitment to him.

Q: What kind of costs might we experience? What about those in other countries around the world?

Jesus ends with a warning. We risk letting difficulties stop us from living distinctively Christian lives. If we do so, we lose our impact on the world around us.

Q: Are you at risk of losing your saltiness? If so, what do you need to do to revive your flavour?

End by praying for those in other countries for whom following Jesus costs a very great deal. You might find it helpful to look at the websites or publications of organisations such as Open Doors or Release International.

3 *Living God's Way*

S ome children long to have control over their own lives. Maybe you were like that, desperate to leave school, to earn your own money, to be able to make your own choices without having to ask for someone else's permission. Others may fear these same things; they rather like someone else taking charge, providing for them and taking the responsibility for decisions. Whatever you felt as a child, in adult life Christians are called to be both independent – responsible for our own actions – and dependent – allowing someone else to take charge and living to please them. The good news is that we don't hand ourselves over to an impersonal corporation or a megalomaniac out to serve themselves, but rather to the one who created us and who longs for us to live the richest life possible.

Setting Out

Q: Have you ever wondered what it would be like to be a completely different kind of person; perhaps an extrovert rather than somebody quiet, a different nationality, tidy rather than messy, calm rather than easily stressed? If you could change one thing about your personality what would it be?

Others might prefer to be somebody else entirely; one of the beautiful people, a superstar musician or a top sportsperson.

Q: You've won a competition and your prize is to choose any celebrity you like and then experience their life for a day. Which celebrity would you most like to be? What attracts you to their life?

Q: What would be the downside of being that person?

Becoming one of Jesus' disciples makes us a new person. That doesn't mean we'll suddenly be unrecognisable, as though we'd had a personality transplant, but people with a different set of priorities in life.

Signposts

As the disciples travelled with Jesus, they discovered more about who he was and the kind of life God wanted them to lead.

THE KEYS TO LIVING GOD'S WAY

1 Realise your own efforts will never be enough

Q: You're reading the paper when your eye is caught by a huge slogan splattered across the page, 'Great results GUARANTEED!' What might this slogan be advertising? What might you have to do to achieve these results?

Q: Have you ever tried something which had such a promise attached? Did it live up to your expectations?

We like to think we can control our lives: if I eat healthily I'll live longer; drive carefully and I'll arrive safely; but we know it doesn't always work out that way. Such hopes aren't new. Here we meet a man who believed that by doing the right things he would guarantee himself eternal life.

Read

Luke 10:25–37

Q: Jesus gives the expected answer to the man's first question so the man then asks a follow-up. What do you think he was expecting Jesus to say here?

As was often the case Jesus did not reply directly to a provocative question but instead drew his listeners into a story.

Q: Imagine you are out and about when you notice a man lying on the ground. What might make someone wary of going to help him?

Q: What might have made the first two men in Jesus' story so unwilling to help the injured man?

Q: How would you describe their attitude towards the man?

Q: Jesus couldn't have used a more extreme example of hatred than the Jews and Samaritans (John 4:9). The idea that the Samaritan would help the Jew would have seemed almost ridiculous to his listeners. Who might replace the Jews and Samaritans in this story if it was told today?

Q: Unlikely it might have been, but it was the Samaritan who stopped to help. How would you describe his attitude towards the man?

Q: What does this story teach us about the true nature of love for others?

Q: Jesus never answers the original question, 'Who is my neighbour?' instead replacing it with, 'Who was the neighbour to the man?' What difference did it make which question was answered?

This parable is a blow to the self-reliant because we can never, consistently, live up to its standards. As Paul reminds us, '. . . all have sinned; all fall short of God's glorious standard' (Romans 3:23). Jesus teaches a vital principle of discipleship through this encounter: that we cannot rely on our own efforts to guarantee eternal life. Obviously, we make every effort to live God's way but the only guarantee of eternal life is Jesus, who said, 'I am the way, the truth, and the life. No one can come to the Father except through me' (John 14:6).

Q: He was such a kind person; he'd do anything for anybody. We all know people who aren't Christians but are like that, don't we? And yet the kindest person you know still hasn't done enough to guarantee their place in heaven. Does that seem fair? Why do you think that such generosity is not enough to get us into heaven?

Q: Maybe there is someone in particular you know to be kind, generous and loving but who doesn't follow Jesus. What do you think Jesus would want to say to them?

2 Get your priorities right

Read

Luke 10:37–42

Q: Your local radio station is running a phone vote. The question is, 'Should Mary get up and help Martha?' How do you think people would vote? How would you vote? Why?

Q: Why do you think Martha thought it was so important to get the meal done?

Q: Was Mary just lazy?

Q: Martha wanted to please Jesus but she went about it the wrong way. Jesus' real desire wasn't for her food but for her heart. Does this mean that the women should have abandoned their responsibilities to spend all their time listening to Jesus?

Q: How might the women have found a better way to balance their need to know Jesus with everyone's need for food?

Q: Why is it sometimes so much easier to do things for Jesus than to spend time with him?

Q: How does the time you give to activity, perhaps especially church activity, compare to the time you give to being alone with Jesus in prayer, reflection or study?

Q: Which comes most easily to you?

Q: Have you got the right balance? If not, what are you going to do about it?

3 Let Jesus into your everyday life

Jesus is our only hope of eternal life and our heart is more important to him than our good deeds. However, we also have a responsibility to live out our commitment in our everyday actions and choices.

Luke highlights money and possessions as one area of life that should reflect our commitment to Jesus.

Read

Luke 12:13–34

Q: This man spent his time and energy on building wealth. Why do you think having so much money made him feel good?

Q: Jesus says the man was a fool for building earthly riches rather than the riches of a relationship with God. Should the man have abandoned his farm and spent the time in prayer instead?

WHAT IS THE BEST WAY TO LIVE?

Read

1 Timothy 6:17,18

1 Seek lasting security in God alone: v 17 (and Luke 12:22–31)

Q: Like the rich man we can seek security in the wrong places, perhaps in money or relationships, a good job or being like our friends. What warning signs will tell us we are replacing God in this way?

Q: What makes you feel secure in life? Is this trust misplaced or not? Are you investing time and energy in knowing God or in things that don't last?

2 Use your gifts wisely: v 18a (and Luke 12:33,34)

Q: What are we to do with our gifts, whatever they are?

Q: Who benefits from your gifts?

3 Share God's attitudes: v 18b

Q: How do you see your money and possessions? Are they:

- the rewards of your hard work;
- yours to put to use as you see fit;
- not enough for your own needs;
- what life is all about;
- something else? What?

How does God see our money and possessions? Psalm 24:1 says, 'The earth is the LORD's, and everything in it. The world and all its people belong to him.' Our possessions are held in trust from God, to be used for his purposes not just our own.

Q: How would you feel if God wanted you to share, or even give away, all but your most basic of possessions? What one possession would you find it hardest to let go of? Why that one?

Q: When might God want us to share (or give away) some of our possessions?

Q: Do you know someone in need at the moment, someone you could help with your money or your possessions? How could you do this?

Q: Think back to the rich man in Jesus' story (Luke 12). How would his actions have been different if he had lived according to God's priorities?

Prayer

Read the introductory words, then allow time to pray, aloud or silently, at the end of each section. If you are meeting as a group you may like to offer people a chance to share any particular thoughts or concerns raised by the session.

'God saved you by his special favour when you believed. And you can't take credit for this; it is a gift from God.' (Ephesians 2:8)

Think back to the story of the good Samaritan. Ask for God's forgiveness for the times you haven't shown love to others. There may be a particular situation or person that comes to mind.

Give thanks for the gift of Jesus, who guarantees eternal life to those who follow him.

'Whatever we do, it is because Christ's love controls us. Since we believe that Christ died for everyone, we also believe that we have all died to the old life we used to live. He died for everyone so that those who receive his new life will no longer live to please themselves. Instead, they will live to please Christ, who died and was raised for them.' (2 Corinthians 5:14,15)

Q: Is pleasing Jesus really the first priority in your life? Ask God to help you see your life through his eyes. Are there things that need changing so Jesus really does come first?

Pray that God will give you the strength and the courage to live his way in every area of your life from now on.

Further Afield

1 FIRM FOUNDATIONS

Read

Luke 6:46–49

Q: Do you like the sea? Do you plunge into the water or paddle tentatively on the edge (or even watch from the safety of the sand)? Our response to Jesus can follow the same kind of patterns; some are wholehearted followers, others prefer to just dip a toe in the water. At first glance we may well not be able to tell the difference; both groups may be in church on a Sunday, on a committee, visiting the sick . . . What about you? Are you wholehearted or dipping that toe in?

Q: Jesus says that the true test of faith is when trouble comes. Under pressure our faith proves itself or can collapse altogether. Maybe you've seen that happen to people you know, maybe it's happened to you.

What does Jesus say makes the difference between faith that lasts and faith that collapses? Why is that?

Q: Pray for those you know who are facing trouble. Pray that God will sustain them and this time may even deepen their relationship with him. How can you support and encourage them at the moment?

2 A STEP TOO FAR

Read

Matthew 19:16–23 and Matthew 13:44–46

Does your church demand that new followers of Jesus should sell all their possessions and give the money to the poor? Even Jesus himself didn't usually make such demands; when he called Peter and the other disciples for example he didn't ask them to do this.

In Matthew 19 we see a man who has obeyed the commandments all his life and yet Jesus asks him to do one more thing before he can become his follower.

Q: Why do you think Jesus makes such a demand on this man?

Q: Do you think every wealthy person has to do this to follow Jesus? Why?

Q: This man decided the cost of following Jesus was too great for him, at least at this point in his life. How is this different from the men described in Matthew 13?

Jesus makes it clear that however good a life we lead, he must be our first priority.

Q: Do you believe that Jesus really is worth giving up everything to follow? Does your life reflect that?

Pray for the help and courage to be wholehearted about following Jesus.

3 BE READY

Read

Luke 12:35–48

Q: Jesus is coming back! What does it mean to be ready and waiting for his return?

Q: Sometimes although we believe Jesus will return one day, we live as though it's not going to happen any time soon. What happened to the servants who lived that way? Why?

Q: If you knew Jesus was going to come back a week today, would you change the way you live during this last week? Why?

Pray that you would learn to live every day as though Jesus was coming back tomorrow.

4 *Under Pressure*

A failure; weak; lets you down in a crisis – would you like to be described that way? Perhaps you would prefer to be known as brave, trustworthy and successful? No contest here; we all want to be well thought of. However, if it matters too much to us, we can end up trying to hide our failings from others, from ourselves and even from Jesus himself. You might wonder whether salvaging a bit of pride in this way really matters, but in hiding our failings it becomes very hard to learn from them and start again. Here we're going to follow the experiences of two men who failed and whose lives were changed forever by the way they dealt with that failure.

Setting Out

You've accepted a new job as Trainee Chief Executive with a huge multi-national company. The night before you start you lie in bed dreaming of your top of the range company car; the vast, beautifully equipped office; the salary; the interesting tasks; the world travel . . .

The next morning you arrive in your smart new suit, ready to go. You meet your training officer and they give you a tatty blue overall and a mop. Your office is a cupboard, your transport the bus, and the task is to clean the floors and make the tea. You realise you should have asked a few more questions at interview. In this company you work your way up from the bottom and it's going to take a while!

Q: How do you think you would feel at the end of your first day?

Q: Why was there such a mismatch between your expectations and the reality?

Q: Have you ever found yourself in a situation where a job or a course didn't turn out to be anything like you had expected? What did you do?

Life doesn't always work out as we hoped, sometimes for reasons beyond our control and sometimes because of our own actions, deliberate or not. Here we see how the actions of two disciples brought them disappointment and failure, but what really made the difference was what they did about it.

Signposts

JUDAS

Read

Luke 22:1–6,21–23 and 45–53

Things definitely weren't turning out as Judas had hoped. Like many of his day, Judas believed the Messiah would overthrow the Roman occupation and lead a restored and independent Israel. The more time Judas spent with Jesus, the more he realised Jesus wasn't fulfilling those expectations at all.

In Acts 1:17 Peter describes Judas as 'one of us, chosen to share in the ministry with us'. Judas had the same opportunities to know Jesus as the other disciples but now he was not happy. Many have speculated as to his motives for betraying Jesus: maybe anger and frustration; maybe a hope he would force Jesus into triggering a revolution at last; maybe a belief that Jesus wasn't the Messiah after all. Whatever his reasons, Luke tells us that Judas made a deliberate choice to hand Jesus over to the authorities (22:4).

Q: How else could Judas have dealt with his dissatisfaction?

Q: 'Satan entered into Judas' (22:3). Does that mean that Judas was responsible for his actions or not? Why do you say that?

Q: How did Satan find a way into Judas' life in the first place? (You might like to read Ephesians 4:26,27 and 2 Corinthians 4:4.)

Q: If the general expectation was for a revolutionary messiah, why did the other disciples not follow Judas into frustration and betrayal?

Despite all he had seen Judas chose to pursue his own dreams rather than commit himself to Jesus. He is a reminder to us that being around other followers of Jesus doesn't automatically mean we will live God's way.

Q: What is it that makes someone into a true follower? Is that true of you or not?

PETER

Read

Luke 22:31–34 and 54–62

Q: Peter believed himself ready to go to prison and die with Jesus. Why was he so wrong about himself?

Judas and Peter were both vulnerable to Satan. Later Peter wrote from experience saying, 'Be careful! Watch out for attacks from the Devil, your great enemy. He prowls around like a roaring lion, looking for some victim to devour' (1 Peter 5:8).

Q: What was it that made Peter particularly vulnerable to Satan's attack here?

Paul says, 'If you think you are standing strong, be careful, for you, too, may fall into the same sin. But remember that the temptations that come into your life are no different from what others experience. And God is faithful. He will keep the temptation from becoming so strong that you can't stand up against it. When you are tempted, he will show you a way out so that you will not give in to it' (1 Corinthians 10:12,13).

Q: Did God give Peter a realistic way out? How could Peter have avoided denying Jesus?

Q: Have you experienced God showing you a way out of temptation? Did you take it up?

Q: Have you experienced times when you couldn't see any way out of temptation? If so, why do you think that was?

Peter realises he is not the man he thought he was; but here there doesn't seem to be such a big difference between Judas, the betrayer and Peter, the denier: they both let Jesus down. The difference comes in what they did about it. One would go on to preach a great sermon and become the rock on which the church was built; the other's remorse didn't lead him into reconciliation with Jesus but to his death.

DEALING WITH FAILURE

Even when it's our own sin that brings about failure we can still move on. How?

1 Realise that every sin can be forgiven

Judas deliberately chose to betray Jesus; Peter found that he wasn't strong enough to do the right thing. Whether sin is deliberate or not, the Bible tells us it can be forgiven. David, king of Israel, committed cold-blooded, premeditated murder to get his own way, incurring God's great displeasure (1 Samuel 11). Despite that sin, God forgave him and he is remembered as a king who served God wholeheartedly. True repentance brings God's forgiveness.

Read

1 Samuel 12:13 and Psalm 32:5

Q: Why did God forgive David?

Judas

Read

Matthew 27:3–5

Q: How did Judas react when he realised what he had done?

Q: Is there a difference between remorse and repentance?

Q: If Judas had really been repentant, what do you think he would have done differently?

Peter

Read

Mark 16:7 and Luke 24:34

Q: Unlike Judas, Peter faced up to his failure. What encouraged him to do that?

Q: What makes it hard to admit our failures to others?

Q: Do you think Peter found it easy to admit his denials? Would you have been as brave as Peter?

2 Repentance brings restoration

Sin breaks our relationship with Jesus; it separates us from him in a way that nothing else can. Peter's experience shows us that repentance is the key to restoring that relationship.

Read

John 21:15–19

Jesus calls Peter to commit himself to serving him, whatever the cost.

Q: Why do you think Peter was upset that Jesus asked him this question so many times?

Q: Why do you think Jesus felt it necessary to keep asking?

Q: How did this encounter restore their relationship?

Peter really meant what he said to Jesus, he wasn't just telling him what he wanted to hear.

Q: How serious are you about loving Jesus? Will you really follow him whatever it costs?

Q: Life is going to throw many challenges at us. How can we find the strength we need to live up to our promise to follow him?

Repentant, restored, renewed

Jesus told Peter he would be the rock on which Jesus would build his church (Matthew 16:18). Jesus saw beyond the sometimes weak and impetuous Peter before him to the future Peter who would be a wise and courageous leader. Here, Peter's restored relationship with Jesus gives him a new start. He learned from his mistakes, changed the way he acted and paved the way to become the rock Jesus had seen so long before.

Q: What attitudes help us to learn from mistakes?

Q: Is there an area of your life where you keep making the same mistake? What does God want you to learn here?

Q: How can Peter's experience encourage us when, like him, we fail to live as Jesus wants?

Prayer

1 Repent

Spend a few moments silently considering whether you see your failures as a chance for growth and a new start or as something to hide.

If you are meeting with a group then divide into two and read these verses from Psalm 32:3–7 (with the second group reading the words in italics).

'When I refused to confess my sin, I was weak and miserable, and I groaned all day long. Day and night your hand of discipline was heavy on me. My strength evaporated like water in the summer heat.

Finally, I confessed all my sins to you and stopped trying to hide them. I said to myself, "I will confess my rebellion to the Lord." And you forgave me! All my guilt is gone.

Therefore, let all the godly confess their rebellion to you while there is time, that they may not drown in the floodwaters of judgement.

For you are my hiding place; you protect me from trouble. You surround me with songs of victory.

Now, silently confess your sins and ask for God's forgiveness.

2 Continue by giving thanks for the good things God gives to us. Begin with these words:

'Oh, what joy for those whose rebellion is forgiven, whose sin is put out of sight! Yes, what joy for those whose record the Lord has cleared of sin, whose lives are lived in complete honesty!' (Psalm 32:1,2).

If you are meeting with a group who aren't very confident with praying aloud, then why not allow a few minutes for people to write down short prayers of thanksgiving and then give people the opportunity to read them out.

3 End by praying for help and courage to live God's way in the future, again beginning with these words:

'The LORD says, "I will guide you along the best pathway for your life. I will advise you and watch over you. Do not be like a senseless horse or mule that needs a bit and bridle to keep it under control.

Many sorrows come to the wicked, but unfailing love surrounds those who trust the LORD. So rejoice in the LORD and be glad, all you who obey him! Shout for joy, all you whose hearts are pure!' (Psalm 32:8–11).

Further Afield

1 A GENEROUS HEART

Read

Luke 15:11–32

Q: The younger son chose to live in a way that led him into disaster. Why was his father's welcome home so generous?

Q: Does it really matter then if we go our own way for a while? After all, we're guaranteed a warm welcome home in the end aren't we?

Q: Maybe we sympathise with the older brother's reaction to his brother's warm welcome. He'd been working hard whilst his selfish younger brother had been away blowing the cash and taking no responsibility for anything. Why was his attitude wrong?

Q: Who do you think Jesus wanted us to imitate in this story?

Q: Do you resemble the father or are you really more like one of the others?

Pray that you would be as generous to those who fail and repent as the Father is to you.

2 UNEXPECTED GUESTS

Read
Luke 14:15–24

Q: Do you enjoy throwing parties? Have you ever hosted a party where nearly everybody dropped out at the last minute? Whether you have or not, how would you feel if it did happen to you? What would you do?

Q: I guess most of us wouldn't choose to fill our party with people dragged in off the streets, especially not the least popular members of society, here the poor and the sick. Why didn't the party just get postponed to another time?

Q: Obviously we don't have to be either poor or sick to be welcome at Jesus' feast table. What was it that really made the difference between those who were at the feast and those who weren't?

Q: Do I sometimes use excuses to put off listening to, or obeying, God? Why isn't that a wise move?

Q: Sometimes we fear that obeying Jesus is going to leave us worse off than doing our own thing all along. How does this story reassure us that this isn't the case?

3 TRUE STRENGTH

Read
2 Corinthians 12:4–10

The gym. Some spend a lot of time there, others spend a lot of time for the first two weeks every year and others would never go near one. Which is most like you? Whatever, most of us probably like the idea of being fit and strong, even if we don't want to have to work hard to achieve it.

Sometimes that desire to be strong stretches into our spiritual lives too: we like to think that our own efforts will make us strong enough to face anything God throws at us. Here Paul shows that that isn't always going to be the case – even he wasn't able to cope easily with everything life threw at him. For Paul, the same problem kept on recurring and prayer didn't bring the hoped-for relief.

Q: How do you react when that happens to you?

Q: We might assume that God's power and a fully fit and vigorous Paul would be the most effective combination, but here Paul says that's not the case, that God's power works best in him when he is weak. Why is that?

Paul didn't allow weakness to overwhelm him or make him resentful. Instead he was glad because it encouraged him to rely on God's power instead of his own, making him a more effective servant. Pray that God might help you develop Paul's attitude to weakness and difficulty in your own life, however far away that might seem at the moment.

5 The Day Everything Changed

*M*any days have a claim to have changed the world: the day JFK was assassinated; the days that have begun and ended wars; the dropping of the Hiroshima bomb; 9/11 . . . Whilst certainly dramatic and life-changing for some, maybe such days don't quite live up to the claims made for them. After all, within a short time most people around the world will have found life continuing much as it did before. However, there was one day that really did change everything for everyone for ever, although, perhaps surprisingly, even those closest to the events of the day took a while to realise things had changed.

Setting Out

The idea of the game is to pass a small object, such as a coin, around the group, without the 'finder' spotting who has it as it goes round.

Choose one brave person to be the finder, who goes out of the room for a few moments. Those remaining sit or stand fairly close to one another. One person has the coin and conceals it from view. The finder comes back and stands in the middle of the group.

When the finder is ready, the object is passed on from the start so that it goes right round the group once. If the finder thinks they know where the coin is they make a challenge. If they are right they join the circle and someone else goes out. If they are wrong they continue as the finder. If the coin makes it right round the circle and back into the possession of the starting person then the group win.

The finder cannot go out of the circle or try to grab the coin and can only challenge three times (to stop random guessing!).

Q: What clues is the finder looking for?

Q: How successfully did the group hide the coin from the finder?

Q: As a group were you better at finding or hiding? Why was that?

Q: Probably all of us have hidden the truth from others at times, even over routine events in our lives. As a child maybe you didn't reveal the full truth over a fight, something getting broken or a school report, for example. Can you remember a time when you did at least try to hide such truths from someone? Were you successful? If not, what gave you away in the end?

Q: Adults aren't immune from keeping routine details of their lives secret, for example their age, weight or salary. Does such secrecy matter? Why?

Signposts

Read

Luke 23:50 – 24:12

The truth about Jesus' death and resurrection was not clothed in secrecy and yet on that first Easter morning none of his followers were expecting anything dramatic to have happened.

Q: What do you think the women expected to happen at the tomb that morning?

1 A SERIES OF UNEXPECTED EVENTS

An open tomb, a missing body, strangers hanging around outside and, Matthew tells us, guards lying unconscious on the ground (Matthew 28:4). It sounds a bit like the ingredients of a thriller doesn't it! Clearly, something very strange was going on.

Q: Imagine the women had turned up at the tomb half-expecting Jesus to have risen from the dead. How do you think they would have reacted when they found his body gone?

Q: How did they really react?

Q: What about the men? They were very dismissive of the women's report. Why do you think both groups reacted as they did?

Job sums up common expectations in the face of death when he says, 'But when people die, they lose all strength. They breathe their last, and then where are they? As water evaporates from a lake and as a river disappears in drought, people lie down and do not rise again. Until the heavens are no more, they will not wake up nor be roused from their sleep.' Job 14:10–12. All Jesus' followers were working on the basis that dead means dead. They had no idea at all that something else might have happened. And yet:

Read

Mark 8:27–31, 9:30–32 and 10:32–34

Q: Jesus had often spoken about his death and resurrection but clearly they hadn't got the message. Why do you think that was?

Q: It takes the reminder of two men 'in dazzling clothes' to bring Jesus' words back to the women. That morning the impossible has suddenly become possible. How do you think the women were feeling on their way back to find the others?

2 THE JOURNEY OF DISCOVERY

Read

Luke 24:13–35

Q: How had Cleopas and his companion responded to the events of the past few days?

Q: The two knew about the events at the tomb that morning. Why then were they still so sad?

For Cleopas and his companion, these events saw all their hopes dashed, but, once again, those hopes came out of their own expectations. In reality everything that happened had been moving God's plans forward. Now, two things combine to bring sense out of their confusion; first, Scripture is explained to them again (vs 26,27) and secondly, crucially, it is Jesus who explains it. Slowly understanding dawns.

Q: Inevitably everyone faces times when events feel meaningless and our hopes and expectations aren't met. What can we learn from the experience of Cleopas and his companion to help us in such times?

Q: How quickly do you turn to Jesus for help in times of trouble?

Q: How can turning to Scripture help us to cope with difficulties in life?

Q: Can you remember a time when reading a particular part of the Bible helped you through a difficult time, or helped make sense of things? What did you read? How did it help you?

Jesus seems to be going to walk on past Emmaus but, as it is late, he's invited to stay. As they eat, Cleopas and his companion realise they have been speaking to Jesus all along. Then, he disappears! Do you think they *ran* back to Jerusalem? At the end of their journey home, they had discovered the truth that Jesus is alive.

Q: Jesus rising from the dead was not meant just to convince his followers he really was the Messiah. Why was it essential for him to die and rise again?

3 HOPES CONFIRMED

Read

Luke 24:35–43

Q: What a rollercoaster of a very long day! What emotions have this group of people been through during the day?

Q: And now, fear, joy, doubt and wonder all combine (vs 37, 41). They knew Jesus had appeared several times that day. Why do you think they were still afraid when he arrived here?

Jesus is a real, physical being and yet he is also changed. Much as we might like the idea, we certainly can't disappear and reappear at will! And yet he's no ghost, no hallucination; the disciples can reach out to touch him and can watch him eat.

Q: We haven't met the physical, resurrected Jesus as they did. How then can we be certain he is still alive today?

All their expectations had been turned upside down. But one question still remains: why? What has it all been for?

Read

Luke 24:44–49

Q: This privileged group of people, the first to see and understand that Jesus really was the Messiah, now have a purpose to fulfil. What are they called to do?

Q: Why couldn't they just sit back, glad that the Messiah had come at last?

As Jesus' followers, we share that same purpose.

Q: How can we play our part today:
- as individuals?
- as a church or group of churches?

Prayer

If you are meeting as a group, then have one person lead this reflection, reading the lines in italics and allowing time for reflection after each section.

Begin with a few moments of silence and then read these verses from Luke:

'That same day two of Jesus' followers were walking to the village of Emmaus, seven miles out of Jerusalem. As they walked along they were talking about everything that had happened. Suddenly, Jesus himself came along and joined them and began walking beside them. But they didn't know who he was,

because God kept them from recognising him. "You seem to be in a deep discussion about something," he said. "What are you so concerned about?"' (Luke 24:13–17a)

Imagine you are walking along, thinking about your current concerns in life. If nothing particular comes to mind then ask God to show you what he wants you to bring to him now.

How are you feeling as you walk? Are you worried, upset or angry? Joyful, doubtful, apprehensive? **(pause)**

As you walk along, Jesus joins you and asks you the same question he asked on the road to Emmaus, 'What are you so concerned about?' What do you say to him? **(pause)**

What do you need from Jesus now? Do you need guidance, understanding or wisdom? Do you need to see the situation through his eyes? **(pause)**

Now ask him what he wants to say to you and listen for his answer. **(pause)**

After Cleopas and his companion had realised it was Jesus speaking to them, they went back to Jerusalem to share their experience with the others. What do you need to do next? **(pause)**

You might like to end this time by singing or listening to a suitable song.

Then, if you are meeting as a group, give people an opportunity to share anything God said to them, or explain any prayer needs.

End by praying together, particularly for anything raised by the group. Pray that we would all share our concerns and lives with Jesus and seek his wisdom and guidance.

Further Afield

1 DOUBTS

Sometimes it's hard to trust other people's word for things even when we know they wouldn't lie to us; we just need to see it for ourselves. Have you ever found yourself in that kind of situation?

Some of us are naturally pretty sceptical about things, not easily convinced by someone else's claims, where others are more trusting. Amongst the disciples, one in particular is remembered for his scepticism.

Read

John 20:24–29

Q: Why do you think Thomas doubted the word of the other disciples?

Q: Notice that whilst Thomas had doubts, he obviously didn't separate himself off from the other disciples but continued to spend time with them. Why was that important?

Q: How did Jesus respond to Thomas' doubts? Why do you think he wasn't angry?

Q: Do you experience doubts about Jesus? If so, what would be a good way to respond to them?

Q: Pray for anyone you know who has doubts about the truth of Jesus. How could you encourage and support them through this time?

2 IN GOD'S TIMING

Read

Acts 1:1–11

Can you stand in a queue without tapping your feet or checking whether you'd have been better off in another line? If you want something, do you want it now or can you put it out of your mind and wait patiently? Patience isn't perhaps the first quality we'd associate with Peter, and it often wasn't too prevalent amongst the other disciples either. Here they demonstrate that impatience once more, as they hope for Israel's physical freedom and the restoration of the kingdom. (You might also like to look at Luke 9:46–48 and 22:24, where the disciples show they misunderstood the nature of God's kingdom.)

Q: Why do you think the disciples kept on asking this question?

Q: Jesus reminds them that everything comes according to God's timing, a timing he isn't necessarily going to reveal to us. However, Jesus didn't keep the disciples completely in the dark. What did they find out about God's purposes?

Q: Why do you think Jesus told them some things about the future and not others?

The disciples did have a part to play in God's purposes, even though at the time they couldn't see exactly how they fitted into God's overall plan.

Give thanks that God has a part for everyone to play, including you. Commit yourself to serving him faithfully, to playing your small part in bringing about his purposes for all creation. You might also like to thank God for others who play their part faithfully and, in so doing, make a difference to your life.

3 JUST A FORETASTE

Have you ever watched a trailer for a film or TV series and then been disappointed by the reality? Maybe you feel that you've seen the only good moments already and are afraid that the full version may bear no resemblance to the trailer at all! A trailer is meant to tempt us, to draw us in on the promise of better things to come, even when such promises are false.

Maybe sometimes we can feel a little as though we have been shortchanged by God's promises too. Jesus died and rose again and yet in the reality of life we still sin and we still suffer. Life can seem to go on much as before.

Read

Romans 8:23–25.

Paul reminds us that what we experience now is, like a trailer, just a foretaste of what is to come and, like all trailers, this one doesn't give us the full picture. The good news is that God's final plans for us are far better than anything we can imagine, anything we experience now. Paul calls what is coming 'a rich and glorious inheritance' (Ephesians 1:18).

Read

Revelation 7:15–17 and 21:2–4

Q: Spend some time rereading these verses from Revelation. What are you most looking forward to in the new heaven and new earth God promises to his people?

Pray that God will give you the strength to wait patiently for his promises to be fulfilled and the courage to look forward with hope, even in the darkest of times.

6 *The Future Begins Here . . .*

*H*ave you ever looked around at the people you're with and wondered how such an oddly assorted group could ever have found themselves together? In occasional quiet moments surely the disciples must have done just that, as they reflected on the unexpected events that led them to follow Jesus. It's easy to look back but maybe if the disciples could have seen into the future they would have been even more surprised. The greatest transformations still lay ahead, as this group of very ordinary people became the leaders, teachers and missionaries in the young church.

Setting Out

Q: It's already possible to book suborbital flights that enable you to experience weightlessness. Soon companies plan to offer public flights into space. If you won a free trip, would you go (health and other considerations permitting)?

Q: Such things sound like the stuff of science fiction, and yet science fiction isn't always good at predicting the future. Have you read books or seen films that had a very strange idea of what the future would look like?

Q: Why do you think people who write about the future sometimes get it very wrong?

Q: What if someone asked you to predict how the world would be different in 20 years time? What inventions would you expect to find? Would you expect other things to have changed too?

Q: What might give us clues about what the future will be like?

Q: Do you find thoughts about the future exciting or not?

Signposts

In this last session we look at the beginning of the church. The disciples can't possibly have understood just what the future held for them as they began to share the good news of Jesus with the world.

Read

Acts 1:14,15; Acts 2:40–47; and Acts 4:1–4

Q: Imagine that within the next few weeks so many new people start coming along to your church that it is a hundred times bigger than it is now, and all these people are new Christians. Why would this be good for your church?

Q: So many new people would inevitably create some problems as well. What might those include? How might your church overcome them?

Q: Do you think you would be glad if this happened or not? Why?

Q: The early church made just this kind of impact in Jerusalem. How did they cope with such rapid growth in their numbers?

The church was exploding in size; Peter, John and the other disciples were out on the streets preaching and working miracles; and yet, just a few months earlier, they had scattered in fear of their lives. Even after the resurrection there were still a relatively small number meeting together.

FOUR THINGS THAT BUILT THE CHURCH

1 The Holy Spirit

Read

Acts 2:1–13

Q: Sounds like a pretty memorable meeting doesn't it! How do you think the disciples felt as the wind and the flames started up around them?

Q: From this time on the disciples were changed people. Why did this experience make such a difference?

Q: The coming of the Holy Spirit obviously made an impact not just on those at the meeting but in the streets round about. How did the people outside respond to what was happening?

Q: What if Peter hadn't gone out to explain what was going on? How do you think those outside would have remembered the day?

Q: And how do you think they would have viewed Jesus' followers after that?

The Holy Spirit's coming was a crucial factor that underpinned everything else that followed but, by itself, wasn't enough to build a growing church.

2 Going into action

Q: What did the disciples do next after the coming of the Holy Spirit? Did they:

- go home on a high;
- write a report about it for the local church magazine;
- arrange extra meetings in the hope it would happen again;
- chat about it afterwards with the others who were there;
- show off to their friends;
- other? What?

Q: Why did they respond as they did?

Q: What difference would it have made if they had followed one of the other possibilities above?

Q: How do you think most churches today would respond to such a dramatic event? Why?

Paul says, 'And now you also have heard the truth, the Good News that God saves you. And when you believed in Christ, he identified you as his own by giving you the Holy Spirit, whom he promised long ago' (Ephesians 1:13). He reminds us that we too have the Holy Spirit at work in us, although we may not have had such a dramatic experience of his coming and presence. Like Peter and the other disciples we are all called to share God's good news with others. If we feel inadequate for such a challenge, we can be reassured that we don't have to go it alone; if we ask, God will provide all the resources we need (Luke 11:5–13).

Q: Does that mean we should be out preaching on the streets as Peter did? If not, what does it mean?

3 A different kind of life

Read

Acts 2:41–47 again, plus Acts 4:32–37 and 5:12–14

Q: What did Jesus' followers share together?

Q: How did those on the outside view the early church at this time?

Q: To be a member of the early church required a huge commitment from its members and not just in time. Would you have liked to be a part of that church? Why?

Q: Whether you would have enjoyed early church life or not, joining it was never an easy choice. Acts 5:14 says people were afraid of joining the church. Why might they have been afraid? (Reading the rest of chapter 5 might give you some ideas.)

Q: How important do you think the lifestyle of the early Christians was in encouraging people to join the church?

Q: How influential is our lifestyle in bringing people into the church today? Why?

Q: Would we make more impact on society if our lifestyle was similar to that of the early church?

If so, is it possible for us to live that way? What realistic changes could we make?

If not, why not?

4 Perseverance

Read

Acts 8:1–8

Despite the difficulties of Christian life in Jerusalem, the church was thriving. Then, suddenly, the persecution becomes so great that the majority of the believers have to leave.

Q: Imagine you are at a prayer meeting in Jerusalem a few days after this wave of persecution began. What do you think the believers would have been praying for?

Q: What ultimately made this persecution a good thing for the church, despite the suffering of individual believers? What might have happened if it hadn't taken place?

Q: Do you think God was glad the persecution broke out in Jerusalem? Why?

The Holy Spirit, the disciples' obedience, the attractive lifestyle, were all essential to the growth of the early church. However, it still might not have lasted if everyone had given up when they were scattered and separated from one another by persecution. Instead, out of their suffering, came the opportunity to share God's good news far beyond their own homes, beginning a process that saw the gospel spread around the whole world.

Q: When you look at these four elements that came together in the early church, do you think they are all equally at work in your church? If so, is that resulting in growth? Why do you think that is?

Q: If you had to pick one, which one would you say is most easily overlooked in your church? Why is that?

FINALLY

We began this series with 12 ordinary men called to follow Jesus. A few years later, we see that same group are leaders of the growing church, leaders of something that was starting to change the whole world. Encountering Jesus changed their lives to a degree they could never have imagined on the day they chose to follow him.

Q: As you look around your church, do you see people whose lives are being transformed by Jesus too?

Q: What about you? Has following Jesus made a real difference to your life?

Ultimately it wasn't worshipping or believing in Jesus that changed the disciples, it was their decision to follow Jesus and change their behaviour, their attitudes and their priorities. They didn't always find that easy; they made mistakes; they were slow to learn and they disagreed: things that didn't completely disappear as the church grew. What they did know was that Jesus was always with them, guiding and encouraging them, working through them to reach his people and bring them home. Like the disciples, if we choose to live our life under the guidance and power of Jesus, we allow him to transform us into people who play a part in changing the world too.

Prayer

If you are meeting as a group you might like to start by reflecting on what you have learnt, or what has struck you most, during this series of studies. Share your thoughts with the others in the group and then give thanks for these things together.

Continue by praying for your church or group of churches and your local community. What good things can you give thanks for in the relationships between the churches in your area? Are there things that aren't going so well that you could pray for?

Pray also for the people who live in your area who don't know Jesus. How do you reach out to these people to offer them care or to introduce them to Jesus?

You might like to pray for any particular projects or events you are involved with.

End with a few moments of silence. Following Jesus means putting aside our priorities and committing ourselves to living his way instead. If that is what you want, whether you've been a Christian for many years or aren't sure whether you are a Christian at all, then end with this prayer.

Lord Jesus, you have called me to follow you. Today I choose to leave behind my own plans for my life, and commit myself instead to seeking yours. Help me, through the power of your Spirit, to live as you want me to in every area of my life and to be a faithful witness to your world. I choose to follow you, wherever you lead, now and for the rest of my life. Amen.

Further Afield

1 FACING THE PERSECUTOR

Read

Acts 8:1–3 and 9:1–31

Q: Bright lights and a voice from heaven in the middle of a public road; Paul's meeting with Jesus could not have been more dramatic! Why do you think God chose to speak to Paul in this way?

Paul changes from chief persecutor into one of God's most dedicated followers. Unsurprisingly other Christians aren't immediately confident that his conversion is real.

Q: How do you think Ananias felt about Paul before he met him?

Q: It would not seem unreasonable for Ananias and the disciples to be angry with Paul over the harm he had done to their fellow Christians. Why do you think this doesn't seem to have been the case?

Q: Ananias showed both grace and courage in meeting and caring for Paul. Do you have relationships where those qualities are needed? Pray that God would help you show them. Pray also for those who currently face persecution around the world, that they might be able to forgive those who harm them.

2 SECOND CHANCES

Read

Acts 15:35–41

Do you fall out with people? Have sharp disagreements? Or perhaps avoid them by vigorously biting your tongue? Avoidance wasn't an option for Paul and Barnabas; they needed to decide whether John Mark was welcome on their next trip or not.

Q: What impression do you get of the tone of the discussion over John Mark?

Q: Do you think these two men should have been able to reach an agreement or didn't it matter?

Whatever the rights and wrongs of the disagreement, God brought two good things out of it: the development of two ministry teams instead of one, doubling their effectiveness and the eventual maturing of John Mark into someone Paul later described as 'helpful to me' (2 Timothy 4:11).

Q: How do you think John Mark was feeling as he left for Cyprus with Barnabas?

Q: Barnabas saw potential in John Mark despite his previous unreliability, potential he was willing to nurture, even though it meant no longer working with Paul. Have you ever experienced someone giving you that kind of second chance? How did it make you feel? Did you make good use of it?

Give thanks for those who've given you a second (or third) chance in the past and consider whether there is someone you now need to give that same opportunity.

3 ONLY JESUS

Read

Philippians 1:12–30

Q: Imagine you, like Paul here, were imprisoned and facing the possibility of being put to death. How do you think you would be feeling?

Q: And how is Paul feeling? Why do you think that is?

Q: Paul's attitude to his imprisonment reflects his desire to honour Christ in everything he does (v 20). What do you think he means by that?

Q: What then might it mean for us to honour Christ in our lives today?

Q: You might like to end by spending some time in quiet reading through Paul's words in Philippians 1:20–24. How much of what Paul says is true for you?

Pray that God would show you anything in your life that does not bring honour to Jesus and stops you living wholeheartedly for him.

About the author

Kate Hayes, born into a non-churchgoing family in Sheffield, decided to become a Christian aged 12 after being 'dragged along' to a Pathfinder meeting by a friend. After studying Psychology at university, she did teacher training but then found herself working in bookshops and in software testing for the book trade. Since 1994 she's been in Dukinfield, Greater Manchester, where she co-ordinates and writes materials for small groups at St John's Church.

OTHER TITLES by KATE HAYES

A Journey of the Heart
A Pilgrim's Guide to Prayer
A companion to this book, with identical format. If you want to explore what it means to pray with purpose, growing in understanding of and intimacy with your God, this series of six Bible-based studies – which can be tackled in a small group or on your own – will take you on a rewarding journey.
ISBN 1 85999 797 X

The Journey of the Son
The second in this series of studies. Based on Matthew's portrayal of Jesus' road to the cross, these six studies consider the struggles we also face to do God's will. We see how Jesus coped with temptation and emotional turmoil, and stayed the course to the end. Suitable for individual or group use, at Lent or any other time.
ISBN 1 84427 097 1

THE RE:ACTION SERIES – 6 SMALL GROUP RESOURCES

For the tough times
Does God care when I'm hurting?
Whether it's thousands killed in a terrorist attack as you watch on TV, your next door neighbour on chemo for cancer, or your best friend's marriage on shaky ground . . . there's no escaping the issue of suffering. Maybe you want to shout at God that's it's just so unfair! Just what's it all for?
ISBN 1 85999 622 1

Chosen for change
Am I part of God's big plan?
Like it or not, you're living in the 'me' culture. Are you comfortable with going it alone, taking care of 'Number One', cashing in on 'your rights' and turning a blind eye to responsibilities? What about sharing . . . caring . . . belonging . . . teamwork . . . community? Are you ready to serve not self – but society?
ISBN 1 85999 623 X

The possibility of purpose
What's the meaning of my life?
A treadmill existence of deadlines and pressures? Or a kaleidoscope of amazing opportunities? What's your take on daily life? Do you see yourself as a meaningless cosmic dust speck? Or a significant mover in a masterplan? Your 'view affects your motivation, your self-esteem, your priorities, your everyday choices . . .

ISBN 1 85999 620 5

Jesus: the sequel
Is he really coming back?
Appointments, schedules, timetables . . . we live in a time-bound society. It's so easy to live just for the present. Are you ready for the future? Not just your next career move . . . your next property . . . your next set of wheels . . . or even your plans for retirement. But the future that begins when Jesus himself returns!

ISBN 1 85999 621 3

More than fine words
Does my faith impact 24/7?
'Churchgoer' means 'hypocrite' to many people. Yet Christians all agree that to show Jesus to others we need to be people of integrity. Genuine. Real. Is that true of you? Does your day-to-day life reflect the reality of your beliefs? Do you 'walk the talk'? Is what you see, what you get?

ISBN 1 85999 770 8

More than bricks and ritual
Am I a team player for God?
Community is under threat. Contemporary lifestyles work against building relationships. Lives are increasingly independent and isolated. What of the church? Does your life just briefly overlap with Christians on a Sunday morning? Are you missing out on God's vision for us as brothers and sisters? As a family? As a team?

ISBN 1 85999 769 4

Available from all good Christian bookshops or from Scripture Union Mail Order: PO Box 5148, Milton Keynes MLO, MK2 2YX, tel: 0845 0706006 or online through www.scriptureunion.org.uk

SCRIPTURE UNION

USING THE BIBLE TO INSPIRE CHILDREN, YOUNG PEOPLE AND ADULTS TO KNOW GOD